# Project Management for Beginners

## The ultimate beginners guide to fast & effective project management!

GW00671804

# Table of Contents

# Introduction

I want to thank you and congratulate you for downloading the book, *"Project Management For Beginners"*.

This book contains helpful information about project management for beginners. Project management is a very broad skill that can be quite difficult to master. There are many varying types of projects, and depending on experience and expertise, a person may be more suited to a specific type.

However, this book aims to prepare you for any type of project, regardless of the field.

This book breaks down the different areas of project management, and the different structures that you may use. You will learn delegation and management skills, and discover what it takes to develop an efficient and effective team.

At the end of each chapter there is an included a chapter summary to help benefit you in the learning process. This is also a valuable resource if you are referring to this guide during the management of a project.

Project management is a highly valued skill. It takes practice, dedication, effort, and persistence. While there is no way to become a great project manager without actually working as one - studying and implementing the information in this book will give you a great advantage!

Thanks again for downloading this book, I hope you enjoy it!

# Chapter 1: Principles of Project Management

## Basic Information

Today, managers often find themselves working on projects that need to be handled with formalized methodology. This is because the technological advances that are related to businesses demand a change in organizational structures and processes. For a company to survive and prosper in its respective industry, its management and employees should be able to execute projects effectively and efficiently.

As a project manager, you must be knowledgeable about the basic terms and ideas associated with this field. This will allow you to communicate with the people you are working with and achieve your goals for your projects. But before we discuss project management, let's define "project" first.

"A **project** is an endeavor in which human, material and financial resources are used to create a unique result, product or service."

Many companies and organizations have their own definition for this word, which can be quite confusing for beginners. That's why the ability to identify tasks that constitute a project can help you apply proper management.

Projects have three fundamental characteristics, which are:

1

- The goal is to create something of value.
- They have different phases, namely: start point, middle point, and end point.
- They will be considered complete once the end point is reached.

Remember these characteristics as they will help you identify projects.

## Different Project Sizes

Projects come in different sizes. Small projects can be organized and handled by a few people while larger projects may require a big number of people and a dedicated group to manage the activities. As a project manager, you should have the knowledge and skills to handle any project regardless of its size. This book is designed to provide you with the information you need to be successful in project management.

## Projects vs. Processes

All of the activities within an organization can be classified either as a process or a project. A process is an activity that happens continually, and usually involves minimal risk. A project, on the other hand, happens once and entails a higher level of risk.

If we will translate that into an equation, it will look like this:

Projects + Processes = All activities within an organization.

## Different Project Types

There are two major classifications of projects: engineering projects and management projects. Engineering projects include mechanical, civil, and electrical engineering. The final results of this project type are physical objects like bridges, refineries, buildings and reservoirs.

Examples of Management Projects are: development of an IT system, preparations for an event, relocation of the business to a new site and launching a new marketing campaign. These examples illustrate that the goal of a Management Project is to produce an intangible result.

A wide range of organizations undertake this type of project, for example: NGOs (Non-Governmental Organizations) and commercial companies.

However, there are other differences between these two types aside from the nature of their end results. These are the following:

- **Environmental Challenges** – Engineering projects usually encounter environmental issues. This is because their operations are physical in nature. For example, a construction project may be interrupted by bad weather, natural calamities and other unforeseen environmental problems.

  Management projects, on the other hand, are often not affected by these issues since their operations take place in the organization's own premises.

- **Specification of End Results**

  For engineering projects, the final results are commonly specified in great detail before the start of the project. This is because the end results need to comply with existing legislation and quality standards.

This is not the same with management projects, where the exact details of the result may only become clear after some work has been done on the project. The plans and expected results stipulated during the project's initial phase often change as the project progresses.

In general, engineering projects are completely different from management projects, which can cause problems to inexperienced managers. However, this book is designed to provide you with the knowledge you need to effectively manage projects of any type.

## Project Management

The objectives of a project are measured in terms of quality, time and cost. To attain these objectives, a project must be properly managed.

As a project manager, you should consider the **scope** of the project when making decisions. A project's scope is defined as the totality of outcomes, benefits, outputs, and work needed to complete the project.

The scope of a project may change as time passes, so a project manager must constantly monitor its components to make sure that the goals will be achieved.

Project management is considered as the application of skills, techniques, tools and knowledge to achieve the goals of a project. This definition is logical, but it doesn't give us specific information as to what kind of skills, knowledge and tools will be needed to manage a project. To find out the requirements of a project, you should look at it from three different viewpoints:

- The scheduled changes and developments – It is the chronological sequence of activities that will happen during the course of the project. It is often referred to as the project's life cycle.

- Compatibility with the Organization – A project should be well-matched with the skills and experience of the people who will work on it. It is important to define the responsibilities of these individuals to attain optimum productivity.

- The knowledge required to manage the project successfully – In project management, this is referred to as **Project Knowledge Areas**. These are areas of management that can be considered independent. In reality, however, these areas still rely on each other to achieve success.

Looking at projects through these perspectives might be difficult at first, but doing so will help you learn more about the projects you will be working on.

## Organizational Structures

The structure of an organization mostly depends on its day-to-day activities. An organization can be project focused or process focused.

- **Project Focused** - The daily activities of these organizations involve the execution of services or delivery of projects for customers within a given time period. The management structure they employ is intended to handle projects effectively. Also, the people working in these organizations are sometimes assigned to multiple projects.

For example: Software Developers, Marketing Agencies, Consulting Organizations and Construction Companies.

- **Process Focused** - The day-to-day activities of these organizations are focused on continuous delivery of products or services to their customers. The management structure being used by these organizations facilitate efficient distribution of products or services.

   For example: NGO's, Charitable Institutions, Utility Companies and Government Departments.

The most common organizational structure used by project managers is the **Matrix Management**. Large organizations, especially those that have numerous business units and international operations, make use of it.

In this structure, an individual that belongs to a specific department can be assigned to different projects. This means the individual may have to report to several managers while performing his/her role.

To give you a better idea about Matrix Management, we will discuss its advantages and disadvantages.

### Advantages of Matrix Management

- Employees are more satisfied and motivated - This is because employees are encouraged to share information with their managers.

- Better data processing - Since people from different departments work together, an efficient exchange of information takes place.

- The leadership style is democratic - This structure encourages the leaders to communicate with their members and get their input before making plans and decisions.

## Disadvantages of Matrix Management

- Individuals are not recognized - Employees may become reluctant to cooperate if they think that their project-related achievements will not be recognized within their own department.

- Potential conflict between managers - This usually occurs between line and project managers. Project managers usually attempt to reduce the department's billing to the project, while line managers often try to secure the maximum budget for it.

- Concerns regarding allocation of resources – Project managers have a tendency to think that their projects are the most important. They usually forget that line managers have their own goals that must be achieved.

## Roles and Responsibilities

All projects require certain roles and responsibilities. These are: manager, stakeholders and sponsor.

- Manager – They are the person assigned to attain the project's objectives. They have the authority to use the allotted resources up to the limit set in the project details. If the manager thinks that the project cannot be completed within the assigned budget or schedule, they must inform the sponsor so that corrective actions can be taken.

- Stakeholders - These are the people who will be affected by the execution or completion of a project.

- Sponsor – They are responsible for securing the financial resources of the project. They also own the opportunities and risks related to its financial outcome.

## Project Life Cycle

The structure of a project's life cycle is: initiation - planning – execution – closure.

## The Initiation Phase

The goal of this phase is to answer the following questions:

- What is the objective of this project?

- What will the company gain from it?

- What is the timeframe?

- Who will sponsor it?

- Who will manage it?

The answers to these questions are recorded in a document known as the **Project Charter**. The information contained here must be revised regularly. New data will be accumulated as the project progresses, and these must be reflected on the project charter to ensure that the goals and requirements of the project are updated.

## The Planning Phase

This phase aims to formulate a plan that can be used to manage the project. Some people believe that they can only start working on the project once this phase is complete. However, that is incorrect. Planning is a continuous activity, and it changes as the project progresses. It is best to constantly update the plan to ensure that the project will be successful.

The focus of the planning phase is on the creation of a plan regarding the execution of the project and the acquisition of the needed resources.

## The Execution Phase

The tasks are done according to the project plan. The results are submitted to the people responsible for the plan so that they can make changes, if necessary.

This phase has two processes: executing (or "doing"), and monitoring and controlling. These processes are implemented to measure and monitor the execution of the plan.

## The Closure Phase

It signifies the conclusion of the project and the delivery of final results to the stakeholders. This phase includes administrative closure which is the formal dissolution of the project team, the completion of all related documentation and termination of any contract.

## Chapter Summary

This chapter explained why project management is necessary for an organization's growth and survival. It discussed the different project types and the difference between projects and processes. The advantages and disadvantages of Matrix Management were also discussed. It explained the roles and responsibilities of the people involved with the project. Lastly, this chapter introduced the four phases of the project life cycle, which are: initiation, planning, execution and closure.

# Chapter 2: Project Process Groups

You should be familiar with process groups if you want to be a successful project manager. This is because these groups constitute all the phases and activities within every project that you will manage.

There are 5 Process Groups: Initiating, Planning, Executing, Monitoring/Controlling, and Closing. These groups are interrelated and are usually performed in the same sequence. You can use these groups, as well as their constituent processes, as a guide for applying suitable project management skills and techniques.

However, it should be clear that these process groups should not be used as rigid activities that must be performed one after another. Make sure that you review each group regularly because the project environment changes as the project progresses.

By discussing things in terms of process groups, we minimize the potential for misinterpretation. We also get a simplified way of studying the different activities involved.

## The Process Groups at Work

To improve our understanding of these groups, let's consider the following example:

You are managing the construction of a new hospital.

- The project is to construct the new hospital.
- The sponsor of the project is the area health authority.

- The whole construction process is divided into three phases:
  1. Clearing the area
  2. Constructing the buildings
  3. Commissioning the hospital facilities

It is important to note that these phases were not identified based on time or activity sequence, but because they are major parts of the construction process. They are usually done in sequence but they can also overlap.

For example:

The "Constructing the buildings" phase could be started before the area is completely cleared. Also, the hospital equipment could be placed in the area prior to the completion of the project.

When you look at a project this way, you may discover that you can work on each of its phases as separate projects. For example, clearing the area for construction may have its own initiation and execution phases.

In reality, the phases of this kind of project usually happen simultaneously. A manager who is familiar with these process groups will see that there is an organized framework of management being used. However, a person who doesn't have a good grasp of project phases might think that this kind of management is chaotic and disorganized.

Before we move on to the next topic, make sure that you understand this concept completely. Process groups don't have to occur in a sequential manner. Generally, they are used at high levels of project management but they can also be duplicated at lower levels of the project, like the delivery of reports to the manager.

You should consider these process groups as guides that can help you focus on the things that must be accomplished at specific stages of the project. The goal of this book is to assist you in identifying the correct project management process that you should use at any given time.

We will now discuss these process groups in detail.

## Initiating Process Group

The processes included in this group are performed to outline a new project or a new phase of an existing project. Within this group, financial resources for the project are secured and the general scope is defined. Similarly, the stakeholders (or the people that will be affected by the project) are identified so that the end results of the project can be assessed.

All of the information gathered is recorded in the Project Charter. However, you must remember that this document is provisional and you can't consider it as your only guide in managing the project.

When a project charter is circulated, the people who will read it may react in two different ways:

- They will support the project because the company will profit from it, or
- They will turn it down because the benefits are not enough to compensate for the costs that will be incurred.

Because of that, the main goal here is to convince the concerned people that there is a business need. They must be informed that alternative options have been considered, but only the proposed project can take care of the need.

Additionally, the scope of the project and the reasons why it is the best solution must be explained to them.

This group has two processes: development of the project charter and identification of stakeholders.

- **Development of project charter** - this is the creation of a document that contains information regarding the project, like initial scope and requirements, to educate the stakeholders and sponsors.
- **Identification of stakeholders** - this is the process of identifying organizations or groups of people that will be affected by the project's execution or completion. All of the related information such as their involvement, interests, and impact on the success of the project must be properly documented.

Stakeholders are divided into three groups:

1. The people who are directly related to the project.
2. The people who are not related to the project but are affected by the organization's plans and actions.
3. The people who are not related to the project or organization.

You should keep in mind that the Initiation process doesn't have to be involved in the actual creation of the end product. Its goal is limited to the identification of the project's goals and what will be needed to achieve them.

# Planning Process Group

This group provides you with the guidelines for combining the different kinds of planning needed in project management. The processes involved here are performed to establish the scope of the activities, explain and improve the goals of the project, and formulate the best course of action to achieve those goals.

The repetitive nature of planning is necessary because projects often involve varying information and unexpected developments that must be considered as the project progresses. As a project manager, you should know how much time and effort to put into each stage of the planning process. That is a very important skill for you to have.

Insufficient planning causes problems that are pretty obvious, for example: there will be inadequate information to estimate the costs and assess the viability of the project. On the other hand, too much planning can also bring negative effects. It can cause unnecessary delays (known as "paralysis by analysis") and make the project team think that the plan is based on invalid assumptions.

## The Components of the Planning Group

The individual parts of the planning process group are listed below. Use this list as a guide when making plans for your projects.

- Collection of Requirements - this will let you manage the sponsor's expectations as well as the goals of the project.

- Scope Definition - this process gives you the information about the project and its products or results. This type of information is valuable for sponsors and stakeholders.

- Creation of the Work Breakdown Structure - this is where you will break down the project into several sections, allowing easy execution and management.

- Definition of Activities, Arrangement of Activities, Estimation of Resources, and Estimation of Activity Durations – these processes produce a list of activities that are necessary for the project's completion. The details and characteristics of the activities are also defined. Once the details are finalized, these activities will be scheduled into network diagrams, together with the approximate resources needed and the time allotted for their completion.

- Development of the Schedule – this process generates the reference points of the schedule and the information needed to carry out the work. This is a complicated process, so coordination between the members assigned to do it is very important.

- Approximation of Costs – this segment of the planning process group provides the estimated costs for all of the activities and phases. The accuracy and usefulness of these estimates greatly depend on the skills of the project manager.

- Budget Determination – this is where all of the estimated costs are combined to create a project budget. This process generates the documentation of the project funding.

- Creation of Quality Metrics – this process creates the Quality Management Plan that defines the quality requirements and checklists. Environmental factors, potential risks and cost performance standards should be considered when creating this plan to ensure its effectiveness.

- Human Resource Plan Development – the people working on the project should have appropriate knowledge and skills. To achieve this, the management plan defines the skills, responsibilities, roles and reporting relationships of the project members.

- Plan Communications – it is necessary to communicate the details of the plan to the sponsors and stakeholders in a timely manner.

## Executing Process Group

This is the process group where most of the work is carried out. It consists of processes and activities that are defined in the project plan. This group involves organizing human and material resources, as well as combining and performing the activities of the project listed in the management plan.

The main goal of the Executing Process Group is to organize teams so that the tasks can be done effectively and efficiently. It also aims to keep the project on track in relation to its scope and initial goals.

It is important to note that this group is not limited to the creation of final products. It is also directly related to the Monitoring and Controlling Process Group. As the project progresses and the tasks defined in the project plan are accomplished, it becomes important to record all the changes related to the project. These records are utilized to monitor and control the project's performance.

This group is made up of eight processes, which are:

- Project Execution – this process is involved with the execution of the activities defined in the project management plan. The phasing and scheduling information must be as precise as possible because this is the process where most of the project budget will be spent.

- Quality Assurance – this is a crucial part of any project because it ensures that the quality of products and end results meet the criteria set. There are several reasons why quality assurance tests must be done regularly, and these are:

  1. Quality issues can be recorded and solved. This will allow the organization to improve its performance and chances of success when working on a similar project in the future.

  2. Important changes in the project management plan can be made to maintain or improve quality.

  3. Stakeholders and sponsors will be assured that the project is going to be completed within its initial budget and timeframes.

- Project Team Acquisition – this process ensures that the knowledge and skills of the project members match the project's requirements. By clearly communicating project expectations and timeframes, the availability of the required members is also guaranteed.

- Project Team Development – this allows the project manager to assess and improve the competencies of the project members. They must ensure that the people assigned to the team can meet the required level of performance.

- Project Team Management – this process focuses on overseeing and improving the performance of each team member. The project manager needs to give feedback to each individual to avoid conflicts. They also need to manage the project changes to sustain excellent performance.

- Distribution of Information – appropriate information must be regularly communicated to the stakeholders and sponsors. That's why it is important to select the most effective means of communication.

- Management of Stakeholders' Expectations – the stakeholders are an important party in every project, so they should always be taken into consideration. They must be assured that their issues will be properly addressed and that their needs will be met satisfactorily.

- Conduct Procurements – every project needs certain resources. Because most of these resources are from external suppliers, an effective procurement process is needed.

Inexperienced project managers may feel overwhelmed by the numerous details and repetitive processes involved here. However, their understanding of these basic processes will be developed over time.

## Monitoring and Controlling Process Group

The processes involved in this group are performed to track, review and regulate the project's progress and performance. They also distinguish the areas that require changes to the plan, and introduce the corresponding changes.

This group compares the results from the executing processes against the plan. If a difference exists, then a corrective action is taken either to change the way in which the plan is being implemented or change the plan itself. That is important because every piece of information learned from the implementation of the plan must be considered. Plan modifications are sometimes necessary to achieve the goals of a project.

The core principle of this process group is the assessment and comparison of actual results against the planned outcomes. If the progress of the project is significantly slower than what is expected, the underlying causes must be identified so that effective remedial actions can be taken.

## Reporting Mechanisms

These mechanisms are time-sensitive. This is because the usefulness of a report depends on how fast it will reach the intended recipient. If the reporting mechanism is slow, then the project manager will not be able to regulate the project effectively.

The control framework that should be used depends on the project's size and complexity. Also, the extent to which different levels of management are involved in the project must be considered. For example, a short project that is exposed to a high level of uncertainty usually requires a short reporting cycle. On the other hand, a project of a longer duration and relative stability often requires a long reporting cycle.

## Collection of Performance Data

A project's control system should be simple. If data collection processes are complicated, then the costs and chances of failure will both increase. However, the timeliness and precision of the data collection procedures can also be affected by practical issues and the efficiency of the project management staff.

## Controlling Changes

Aside from comparing actual results against the planned outcomes, this process group is also concerned with controlling the changes related to the project and proposing preventive actions in anticipation of potential issues.

There are four major sources of change. These are:

- Technical – technological advancements may offer better solutions or procedures. On the other hand, technical issues may affect the execution of the plan or the quality of the products.

- Environmental – this includes changes in business strategies, legislation, and government policies.

- Organizational – business decisions made by top-level managers may alter some parts of the original project plan.

- End-User – this results from the changes in customers' needs or perceptions.

A project manager must use a process to control these potential changes and their effects. This process should interpret these changes in terms of their potential effect on project quality, benefits, timeframes, personnel and costs.

## Closing Process Group

These processes are performed to close a cancelled project, formally terminate all activities related to a project, or transfer the finished products to the end-users.

The project closure phase must ensure that the project is brought to a planned end, which means:

- All of the contracts established because of the project are terminated formally.

- All of the final products are transferred to the end-users.

- All of the useful lessons acquired from the project are recorded and stored.

## Chapter Summary

This chapter gave a detailed description of the process groups involved in project management. These process groups are: planning, executing, monitoring, controlling and closing. The processes included in each group were also explained.

# Chapter 3: Project Cost Management

The initial step in the cost management process group is to determine the total cost for the project and the accuracy of the estimated costs.

As a project manager, you will make day-to-day decisions based on approximate values. The accuracy of these values can have a huge impact on the outcome of the project. Projects that are launched with an inaccurate initial estimate usually experience serious problems. That means an accurate cost estimate is necessary for a successful project.

Additionally, in certain cases, a project manager may have a legal responsibility for preparing the cost estimates properly. They must document all of the information they used as basis for their cost estimates because their decisions might be challenged later on.

Similar to other processes in project management, cost estimation is repetitive. Also, the more experience you have in doing it, the more accurate and reliable your estimates will become.

There are five questions that you must answer when estimating costs. These are:

- Is the scope clearly defined?

- Are the predicted productivity rates accurate?

- Is the resource availability assumption reliable?

- What factors can affect this estimate?

- How likely are they to happen?

## Project Budgeting

This phase involves acquiring the estimated cost data, determining which cost options to use, computing their effects, and assigning cost information to work packages. The project cost plan should be compatible with the fund distribution method being used for the project.

## Cost Control

This is the final process in this group. The goal of this process is to determine four things, namely:

- The actual costs

- The intended costs

- Why they differ

- What can be done about it

Determining the variance between the actual costs and intended costs is a simple procedure. In fact, there are several tools that can be used to quantify any difference. A project manager must be able to describe exactly where a project is in terms of costs. They are expected to submit a variance report to the sponsor of the project.

The remainder of this chapter will discuss the four processes in Project Cost Management. These are:

1. Cost Management Planning
2. Estimate Costs

3. Determine Budget
4. Control Costs

## Cost Management Planning

This is where the documentation, policies and procedures regarding the project's costs are established. The main goal of this process is to create guidelines for the proper management of costs.

This process has three elements:

- Tools and Techniques - it involves budget planning, analytical techniques and meetings between people assigned to handle the costs of a project.
- Inputs - it involves the project charter, project management plan and all the environmental factors that can affect the project or the organization itself.
- Output - the end product of this process is the cost management plan.

## Estimate Costs

This process is focused on the estimation of costs of all the resources that will be used for the project. These resources are: materials, labor, service and equipment.

Cost estimation during the initial phase of a project can be very difficult, especially if there is little or no historical data that can be used as a basis. There are several tools and techniques that can be utilized to accomplish this task but experience is still very important. Also, the accuracy of these estimated costs improves as the project progresses because more information becomes available.

When estimating costs, it is important to determine if the indirect costs should be included in the estimates. These are the costs that cannot be directly traced to the project. They are also accumulated and distributed across multiple projects by an approved accounting procedure.

This process is composed of three elements:

- Tools and Techniques - it involves analogous estimation of costs. This technique uses the values of time, budget, scope and costs as parameters for the project.
- Inputs - this is composed of cost and human resources management plans.
- Outputs - these are the estimated values that will be used in updating the project plan.

## Determine Budget

This is where the costs are added up to generate an authorized cost baseline. All of the authorized budgets are included in this baseline, except the management reserves.

Similar to the previous processes in this group, budget determination has three elements. These are:

- Tools and Techniques – this process involves the use of historical data from similar projects and the estimated costs indicated in the WBS (Work Breakdown Structure).
- Inputs – the process requires the project scope, cost management plan, project schedule, cost estimates and the basis used in the estimation process.
- Outputs - this process determines the baseline for cost performance and the funding requirements of

the project. These pieces of information will be used to make necessary adjustments in the project plan.

## Control Costs

This is the process where the progress of the project (in terms of its costs) is monitored. This is also where the project manager must update the project budget and manage the changes to the cost baseline.

The elements of this process are:

- Tools and Techniques - the main techniques used in this process are TCPI (To-Complete Performance Index), performance reviews, EVM (Earned Value Management) and forecasting. The tool used here is a project management software.
- Inputs - these are the project funding requirements, work performance information, project management plan and organizational process assets.
- Outputs - the end products of this process are cost forecasts, plan modification requests, and updates to the project management plan.

## Chapter Summary

The processes included in Cost Management are focused on budgeting, controlling, planning and estimating project costs. They ensure that the project can be accomplished within the allowed budget.

These procedures are utilized to generate a budget, and to observe the project's performance in relation to that budget. A project manager must consider the actual and forecasted consumption of resources when updating the project's budget.

# Chapter 4: Project Time Management

Project time management is considered as the fundamental discipline in managing projects. In fact, there is a wide selection of management software tools designed exclusively for this group. This process group is the logical and organized way of executing the project plan.

It's important to note that this group is necessary in all phases of the project's life cycle. This process group is often performed during the initial phase to serve as a framework for the execution of the plan. It allows the project to continuously evolve through the planning, executing and monitoring phases.

This group is composed of seven repetitive processes that can be improved as the project progresses. These are:

1. Management of Plan Schedule
2. Definition of Activities
3. Scheduling of Activities
4. Estimation of Activity Resources
5. Estimation of Activity Time Frames
6. Schedule Development
7. Controlling the Schedule

## Management of Plan Schedule

The primary goal of this process is to establish the policies and procedures that will be used in the execution of the plan schedule. Its elements are:

- Tools and Techniques - the analytical techniques used in this process include: review of schedule performance, analysis of alternatives, schedule compression, leads & lags and rolling wave planning.
- Inputs – this process needs the project charter, organizational process assets, project management plan, and all environmental factors that may affect the project.
- Outputs - it generates the schedule management plan. This plan is used as the framework for the remaining time management processes of the project.

## Definition of Activities

This process identifies the specific tasks that must be accomplished to achieve the goals of the project. During this process, it is necessary to generate sufficient information so that the required time and resources can be estimated. It also has its own set of elements, which are:

- Tools and Techniques - the scope baseline is used as a starting point to divide the project activities and results into their individual components. This is known as decomposition.
- Inputs – this process requires the schedule management plan, enterprise environmental factors and scope baseline. The scope baseline is made up of a scope statement, WBS (Work Breakdown Structure) and WBS dictionary.

- Outputs - this process creates a list of the activities and milestones for the project.

## Scheduling of Activities

After identifying the activities, the project manager must arrange them according to their importance and dependencies. These dependencies must be known because they determine the correct sequence of activities. There are four types of dependencies, which are:

1. Start to Start Relationship - means an activity will only start if another activity also starts.
2. Start to Finish Relationship - means an activity will be finished once a different activity is started.
3. Finish to Start Relationship - means an activity must be finished first before a different activity can be started.
4. Finish to Finish Relationship - means an activity can only be finished if a different activity is also finished.

The dependency of an activity can either be internal or external. For example, a company may purchase raw materials from an outside supplier. The purchase and delivery of these materials represents an external dependency, because a relationship with a supplier not related to the project is established.

This process is made up of the following elements:

- Tools and Techniques - the techniques used in this process are: dependency determination, application of leads and lags and precedence diagram method.

- Inputs – these include the project scope statement, list of activities or milestones and enterprise environmental factors.
- Outputs – the product from this process is a network map showing the arrangement of the activities and their dependencies.

## Estimation of Activity Resources

This is the step where the resources needed to complete each activity are estimated. The processes discussed earlier focused on what is to be done and in what order. This process defines who will perform the tasks.

Keep in mind that you should not worry about the factors that you don't understand. The most important word here is "estimate". Although you should attempt to be as precise as you can, remember that any value or figure you get will be revised later on.

The following list shows the elements of this process:

- Tools and Techniques – the tools used in this process are: analysis of alternatives, bottom-up estimating, project management software and expert judgment.
- Inputs – this process uses the activity list, activity attributes, cost estimates, risk register, resource calendar and the schedule management plan.
- Outputs – this step produces updates to project documents, activity resource requirements and RBS (Resource Breakdown Structure).

# Estimation of Activity Timeframes

This is where the amount of effort needed for each task is estimated, which will be used to compute the timeframes of the project. Effort is measured in terms of the task's difficulty. The timeframe, however, is calculated by dividing the value assigned to effort by the estimated resources.

All estimates are naturally unreliable (to some extent) at the initial phase of the project. They should be gradually revised as you gain more information about the work being done and the resources that you can use.

These are the elements of this process:

- Tools and Techniques – expert judgment, reserve analysis, parametric estimation, and analogous estimation are the tools used in this process. The technique utilized here is the Group Decision Making Technique.
- Inputs – this process uses the project scope statement, resource breakdown structure, resource calendars, schedule management plan, activity list and enterprise environmental factors.
- Outputs – the results from this process are project document updates and activity duration estimates.

## Schedule Development

As the project manager, you should have all the data needed to develop a project schedule at this point. A scheduling tool is often used to complete this process, which can instantly generate results based on:

- Estimated Timeframes
- Defined activities
- Relationships between the activities
- Resource Availability

This process is made up of:

- Tools and Techniques – the tool used here is the scheduling tool. The techniques, on the other hand, are: resource optimization techniques, schedule network analysis, modeling techniques, critical path method and the critical chain method.
- Inputs – this process makes use of schedule management plan, activity list, project schedule network maps, resource requirements, project statement, project staff assignments and resource breakdown structure.
- Outputs – the products are schedule data, project schedule and the schedule baseline.

### Controlling the Schedule

This step is used to observe the status of the schedule baseline and make changes to it if necessary. A schedule baseline must be updated constantly for it to indicate the status of the project.

This is a part of the Monitoring and Controlling Phase and is sometimes called "working the plan". This is in contrast with the preceding processes which are focused on "planning the work".

The "Controlling the Schedule" process is concerned with:

- Checking if the schedule has changed
- Controlling changes as they happen
- Ascertaining the current status of the schedule
- Managing the factors that may cause changes in the schedule

The elements of this process are:

- Tools and Techniques – the tools used here are the scheduling tool, project management software and performance reviews. The techniques used are schedule compression, resource optimization techniques and modeling techniques.
- Inputs – this process uses schedule data, project calendars, project management plan, work performance data and organizational process assets.
- Outputs – these are the schedule forecasts, change requests, work performance information and project management plan updates.

## Chapter Summary

The processes involved in project time management are recorded in the schedule management plan. This plan supplements the project management plan and provides general or detailed information depending on the project's needs.

To develop the project schedule, the outputs from other processes are used. Included here are activity details, activity resource estimates and sequence of activities.

The schedule, once approved and finalized, will be used as the baseline in the execution of other processes. As the project progresses, most of the work in this knowledge area will be reflected in the "Controlling the Schedule" process. It means the activities are completed in a timely manner.

# Chapter 5: Project Communications Management

A project manager's job is not limited to performance monitoring and decision making. They must also communicate with the project members, stakeholders and sponsors. Project members should be informed about the manager's instructions to ensure that the project will be completed successfully.

On the other hand, the sponsors and stakeholders must be updated regularly to set their expectations and assure them that the project is making progress. In order to do these things, the project manager must use an effective form of communication.

Project Communications Management is made up of processes that guarantee timely collection and distribution of project data. Its main goal is to construct a communication infrastructure that allows people involved in the project to get access to the right data at the right moment.

Communication is considered as a common management skill that it is not limited to project management only. Although this is true, projects have specific features that may cause communication issues and therefore require a communication management plan.

Projects usually produce large amounts of information that must be accumulated, organized and examined. An effective communication structure can assist the project manager in keeping these activities under control.

The Project Communications Management is composed of three processes, which are:

1.  Planning Communications
2.  Managing Communications
3.  Controlling Communications

## Planning Communications

This process determines the information needed by project stakeholders and defines the communication approach that will be used. The communications management plan, which is its main product, answers the following questions:

- Who are the stakeholders?
- What are their interests?
- What information do they need?
- What/Who is the source of the information?
- How often should the stakeholders be updated?
- What format of communication should be used?

The elements of this process are:

- Tools and Techniques – the tools used here are communication models and communication technology. The techniques involved are communication methods and communication requirements analysis.
- Inputs – this process needs the project management plan, enterprise environmental factors and stakeholder register.

- Outputs – this process produces project document updates and the communications management plan.

## Managing Communications

This process aims to keep the stakeholders and sponsors updated on the project's progress. It is done in accordance with the communications management plan created in the previous process.

The elements of this process are:

- Tools and Techniques – the tools used here are information management systems, communication models and communication technology. The technique involved is performance reporting.
- Inputs – this process requires the communications management plan, enterprise environmental factors and work performance reports.
- Outputs – the process produces updates for the project management plan, project documents and organizational process assets.

## Controlling Communications

This is the process involved in monitoring and controlling communications to guarantee that the needs of the stakeholders and sponsors are met. It requires regular accumulation and examination of data to share the project's progress with the stakeholders. This process also allows the project manager to forecast future performance.

It is composed of the following elements:

- Tools and Techniques – the tool used here is an information management system. The technique involved is expert judgment.
- Inputs – this process requires the issue log, work performance data, project management plan, project communications and organizational process assets.
- Outputs – the process produces work performance information.

## Chapter Summary

A formal communication plan is an important aspect of project management. It allows effective accumulation, classification and analysis of huge bulks of data and information.

The internal structure of the Project Communications Management Plan guarantees that each individual can access the correct information at the right time so they can complete the task successfully. This is particularly relevant when the project manager is communicating with the stakeholders, updating them and maintaining their support.

# Chapter 6: Project Human Resources Management

This knowledge area is the core of successful project management, because the tasks and activities needed by the project are done by people, not by management methods or computer software. It is obvious that organized knowledge and advanced technology can help, but project management should be focused on managing the people who will do the work.

It aims to educate, lead and manage the project members effectively. In this chapter, we will use the terms:

- "Project management team" – these are the people assigned to manage the project.
- "Team members" or "Project team" – these are the people who are doing the tasks of the project.

The project management team is often a subgroup formed from the project team. This team is responsible for the management of the project and leadership activities.

The number of people working in the project may change, especially when more people are required to handle the technical aspects of a project.

It is advisable to assign the project team as early as possible so that they can contribute in the planning process. Although they are not responsible for planning, some of them may have relevant working experience that can help in generating accurate initial estimates.

Aside from that, involving the team members in the planning process intensifies their commitment to the project. This is very important, especially when problems need to be solved. However, this is often ignored by project managers because it cannot be quantified.

There are four processes included here:

1. Human Resource Plan Development
2. Project Team Acquisition
3. Project Team Development
4. Project Team Management

## Human Resource Plan Development

Every member of a project must have a role and a set of responsibilities. This process defines how the project manager will assess, team build, improve and manage the project team. For that reason, this process is done during the initial phase of the project and is implemented repeatedly as the project progresses.

This process includes the production of project organization charts and schedules for personnel acquisition and release. It may also involve the recognition of safety issues, training requirements, compliance considerations and team-building strategies.

To develop this plan, the project manager must have a detailed description of the activities necessary for the project's success. Because other projects may need the same skills or competencies, the project manager must consider the availability of human resources when creating this plan.

Many project managers use the Matrix or Cross-Functional type of management. This is a system of managing people through a series of relationships. It is very popular in projects that require individuals from different departments (e.g. finance, marketing, sales, etc.) to join the same team. That means these team members must report to two managers: the project manager and the department manager.

As a project manager, you need to make sure that you can communicate with the department manager effectively. Also, you should remember that the priorities of the department manager are usually different to those of your project.

The elements of this process are:

- Tools and Techniques – the tools used here are organizational theory, organization charts and position descriptions. The techniques are networking and expert judgment.
- Inputs – this process requires the project management plan, enterprise environmental factors, organizational process assets and activity resource requirements.
- Outputs – the process creates the HR management plan.

### Project Team Acquisition

This process happens within the executing process group and is involved with the availability of human resources. Its aim is to acquire qualified personnel to complete the assignments required by the project. Individuals with different competencies will be required at different points in the project's life cycle, making this process complicated.

Departmental staff will be acquired based on their skills and expertise. However, their business or technical skills must be accompanied by capacity and willingness to perform in the project. These people will remain under the overall authority of their own line manager but they will report to the project manager, which means they are working in a matrix management environment.

These are the elements of this process:

- Tools and Techniques – the techniques used here are negotiation, acquisition, pre-assignment and multi-criteria decision analysis.
- Inputs – this process requires the human management plan, enterprise environmental factors and organizational process assets.
- Outputs – the process generates resource calendars, project staff assignments and project management plan updates.

## Project Team Development

The objective of this process is to assemble a team that can work effectively and efficiently. Because team building requires a long timeframe, this process should be started during the project's initial phase. Keep in mind that a team that works well together will have a huge impact on the success of the project.

As the project manager, you can develop team performance by developing trust among members of the team, encouraging collective decision-making and problem-solving, using open and effective communication and managing disagreements in a positive manner.

The elements of this process are:

- Tools and Techniques – the tools used here are interpersonal skills, personnel assessment tools, training, recognition and rewards, team-building activities and ground rules.
- Inputs – it requires resource calendars, human resource management plan and project staff assignments.
- Outputs – it produces team performance assessments and enterprise environmental factors updates.

## Project Team Management

Human resource management is one of most difficult knowledge areas because people can be unpredictable. The level of their confidence can go up or down. Also, they can cause unexpected conflicts or even abandon the project in an unplanned manner.

To ensure success, a project manager must have the following skills:

- Leadership
- Communication
- Conflict Management
- Negotiation

This process is composed of these elements:

- Tools and Techniques – the process involves conflict management, interpersonal skills and project performance appraisals.

- Inputs – it requires the issue log, work performance reports, project staff assignments, team performance assessments, organizational process assets and human resource management plan.
- Outputs – it generates change requests and updates for the project management plan, enterprise environmental factors and organizational process assets.

## Chapter Summary

This knowledge area seeks to tackle two main issues:

1. The issue between getting the task done in the shortest time possible and the necessity to improve the skills and competencies of the team members.
2. The issue between choosing and controlling people based on the project's requirements and managing them as individuals with their own personal and professional needs.

As the project manager, you should keep in mind that the success of the project depends on its members. This is because the tasks and activities are done by people. Also, human resource management is a task that you cannot assign to others. You should develop your interpersonal and leadership skills to be an effective project manager.

# Chapter 7: Project Risk Management

A risk is a future incident that may or may not occur. If it does occur, then it will have an effect on the quality, scope, cost or schedule of the project. It is important to remember that all project activities entail some element of risk. Similarly, the difference between project risks and business risks must be understood.

- Project Risk – is a potential condition or event that, if it occurs, has a positive or negative influence on the project's goals.
- Business Risk – is related to the insecurity in earnings or danger of loss of a business.

As a project manager, you should be aware that a risk has two potential effects: positive or negative. That means for every risk involved in a project, there are threats and opportunities that you must assess. Let us discuss these in detail:

- Threats – have negative effects that should be diminished. The project management team must strive to minimize these effects.
- Opportunities – must be grasped because they offer potential benefits for the project. The management team must take actions to make sure that these are achieved.

Stakeholders and sponsors may be willing to undertake risks, depending on their risk tolerance. For example, risks to the project may be accepted if the benefits that can be gained from them outweigh the associated threats.

The risk tolerance of organizations is influenced by their culture and legal status. However, the people's approach to risks is guided by tolerances, insight and other biases.

There are six processes involved here:

1. Risk Management Planning
2. Risk Identification
3. Qualitative Risk Analysis
4. Quantitative Risk Analysis
5. Preparation of Risk Responses
6. Monitoring and Controlling Risks

## Risk Management Planning

This is where the risk management plan is created. This plan describes how risk management will be performed, but it is not involved in the actual identification of project risks.

The type of information needed in the risk management plan depends upon the organization's risk tolerance and the risks involved in the project.

Risk Management Planning is composed of the following elements:

- Tools and Techniques – this process involves analytical techniques and expert judgment.
- Inputs – this process requires the project management plan, risk register, project charter, organizational process assets and enterprise environmental factors.

- Outputs – it produces the risk management plan.

## Risk Identification

This process aims to identify the risks that may affect the project and assess the outcomes should they occur. The data will be recorded in the risk register, which is a list of all the known risks, their main causes, classifications and reactions. Because risk assessment is a continuing task, the risk register must be updated regularly throughout the project's life cycle.

A project manager should encourage all project team members to identify risks. Remember that this is a repetitive process. New risks will be known as the project develops, so everyone involved in the project must have a sense of ownership and accountability for the risks and their potential effects.

The elements of Risk Identification are:
- Tools and Techniques – the process involves checklist analysis, assumptions analysis, documentation reviews, information gathering, SWOT analysis, expert judgment and diagramming techniques.
- Inputs – this process needs the schedule management plan, scope baseline, stakeholder register, procurement documents, quality management plan, risk management plan and human resource management plan.
- Outputs – it produces the risk register. The information contained in this document will be used to develop the RBS (Risk Breakdown Structure).

# Qualitative Risk Analysis

The risks recorded in the register are analyzed in this process. Their probability and potential effect on the project are assessed by the project management team. The results from the analysis are used to assign suitable time and resources to the risks that must be controlled.

Similar to the other processes within risk management, Qualitative Risk Analysis should be done on a regular basis. That is because new risks may be determined and the features of existing risks may evolve throughout the project's life cycle.

The elements of this process are:

- Tools and Techniques – the process involves risk categorization, risk urgency assessment, data quality assessment, probability and impact matrix, and expert judgment.
- Inputs – this process needs the scope baseline, risk register, risk management plan, enterprise environmental factors and organizational process assets.
- Outputs – it produces project document updates.

# Quantitative Risk Analysis

This is the process that assigns numerical values to the identified risks. It is used to evaluate the effects of the risks determined in the qualitative analysis.

It is important to note that some projects can create successful risk responses without this process. A project manager can determine the need for quantitative risk analysis by evaluating the availability of resources and the usefulness of numerical statements.

Quantitative Risk Analysis is made up of:

- Tools and Techniques – this process involves data gathering & representation techniques, modeling techniques and expert judgment.
- Inputs – this process requires the cost management plan, risk management plan, risk register, schedule management plan, organizational process assets and enterprise environmental factors.
- Outputs – it produces project document updates.

## Preparation of Risk Responses

This process aims to develop actions and alternatives to improve opportunities and to minimize the threats related to the project. The planned responses must be agreed upon by all parties involved, and they should be suitable to the nature and significance of the risk. Additionally, these responses should be cost effective and realistic.

The elements of this process are:

- Tools and Techniques – this process involves contingent response strategies, strategies for positive risks, and strategies for negative risks.
- Inputs – this process needs the risk register and the risk management plan.
- Outputs – it generates updates for the project management plan and project documents.

## Monitoring and Controlling Risks

This process has several steps: identification of new risks, implementation of the risk response plan, monitoring of identified risks and assessment of the response plan's effectiveness.

Throughout the project's life cycle, the planned risk responses must be implemented and monitored. That means the project manager must continuously look out for new, evolving and outdated risks.

The elements of this process are:

- Tools and Techniques – the process involves reserve analysis, risk audits, risk reassessment, variance & trend analysis, meetings and technical performance measurement.
- Inputs – the process needs the project management plan, work performance reports and the risk register.
- Outputs – this process creates change requests, work performance information and project management plan updates.

## Chapter Summary

Risks play a major part in the planning phase of any project. As the project manager, you should have a good grasp of the stakeholder's risk tolerance.

The main goal of risk management is to intensify the likelihood and effect of opportunities, while minimizing the influence and probability of threats. You can achieve this by systematically inspecting and defining the constraints, assumptions or conditions related to the requirements and objectives of your project. You should not concern yourself with business risks that affect the organization as a whole.

# Chapter 8: Project Procurement Management

It is rare that a project can be successfully completed without obtaining products or services from external resources. Once the needs of the project are determined, a supplier must be selected so that the necessary materials or services can be acquired.

Organizations normally have standard policies and procedures regarding the procurement of materials from outside sources. Additionally, the members of the project management team may be required to consult the legal representatives of the organization about this knowledge area.

There are four processes included in Project Procurement Management:

1. Procurement Management Planning
2. Operate Procurements
3. Regulate Procurements
4. Terminate Procurements

## Procurement Management Planning

This process aims to determine which materials or services should be obtained from external sources. Once done, the project manager must choose the suitable types of contracts that will be needed for the project.

The choice being made is either "buy" or "create". This choice is affected by the resources that are currently available and the requirements of the project plan.

During this process, the risks involved in each "buy or create" decision must be carefully considered. Also, the project manager needs to review or revise the contracts that will be used with respect to the risks and their potential effects.

Procurement Management Planning is composed of:

- Tools and Techniques – this process involves market research, make-or-buy analysis, meetings and expert judgment.
- Inputs – this process needs requirements Documentation, project schedule, activity costs estimates, activity resource requirements, project management plan and the risk register.
- Outputs – this process generates procurement documents, procurement management plans, procurement statement of work, make-or-buy decisions and the source selection criteria.

### Operate Procurements

This is the process where external suppliers are selected and awarded with contracts. It may happen multiple times, depending on the number of suppliers and contracts involved.

It has the following elements:

- Tools and Techniques – the process involves proposal evaluation techniques, bidder conferences, independent estimates, advertising, analytical techniques and expert judgment.

- Inputs – this process needs the procurement management plan, source selection criteria, seller proposals, procurement documents and make-or-buy decisions.
- Outputs – this process generates resource calendars, agreements, selected sellers, change requests, project document updates and project management plan updates.

## Regulate Procurements

This process aims to monitor contract performance, manage relationships with sellers, control potential changes and take corrective actions when necessary. When transacting with external suppliers, the project management team should consider the legal implications of their actions. It means any change that must be introduced to the contract needs to go through a process called "Project Integrated Change Control". The change is then incorporated into the project management plan itself and is considered as an essential part of project integration management.

The elements of this process are:

- Tools and Techniques – the process involves inspections and audits, performance reporting, payment systems, claims administration, procurement performance reviews, contract change control system and records management system.
- Inputs – the process needs the project management plan, work performance reports, work performance data, approved change requests, procurement documents and agreements.

- Outputs – it produces change requests and work performance information.

## Terminate Procurements

This process aims to complete all project procurements and verify that all the materials or services obtained are of the expected quality. Additionally, it may involve managerial tasks such as updating records to show end results, concluding open claims and storing the useful information for future use.

The elements of this process are:

- Tools and Techniques – the process involves procurement negotiations, records management systems and procurement audits.
- Inputs – the process needs the procurement documents and the project management plan.
- Outputs – the process creates organizational process assets updates and closed procurements.

## Chapter Summary

This chapter defined a verified standard that you can use for the procurement aspects of your project. The processes included in this knowledge area will help you ensure that all project purchases are under your control. They also allow you to establish good working relationships with external suppliers.

As the project manager, your job is to make certain that sufficient time is allotted for the procurement processes. You should let the procurement department handle the day-to-day purchases for your project.

# Conclusion

Thank you again for downloading this book!

I hope this book was able to help you learn more about project management!

Learning about project management, and successfully managing a project are two separate things. However, with the knowledge provided in this book you will be much better prepared to tackle your first project! Good luck!

Finally, if you enjoyed this book, please take the time to share your thoughts and post a review on Amazon. It'd be greatly appreciated!

Thank you and good luck!

Lightning Source UK Ltd.
Milton Keynes UK
UKHW050707030122
396514UK00010B/947